BEARS

Sandie Lee Books

Bears

Bears are big, powerful and hairy mammals that live all over the world. There are 8 species of the bear called, Ursidae. Bears have been around for millions of years, but the first bears did not look like the bears we have today. These animals are thought to have been more raccoon-like in appearance. Like these prehistoric bears, some bears today are in danger of becoming extinct. Let's discover more about the amazing world of bears.

Where in the World?

Did you know that bears live in North and South America, along with Europe and Asia? These burly beasts can be found in forests, frozen tundra and along the alpine scrub. Some bears will wander into cities and like to eat people's garbage, but mostly they just like to be left alone.

The Body of a Bear

Did you know bears can weigh from 100 pounds all the way up to 1700 pounds? The bear has short, stocky legs, a small tail, fuzzy ears and a long muzzle. The paws on a bear are very large. The bottom of the paws have pads and each toe has a long claw.

What a Bear Eats

Did you know even though bears are considered carnivores some actually only eat plants? Bears will climb trees and eat tender shoots, acorns, nuts and berries. Some bears like to eat salmon and other fish, while others even hunt seals. The sloth bear makes its diet on termites and other insects.

The Bear's Special Ability

Did you know bears in the colder regions of the world have the ability to withstand extreme temperatures? They have a thick coat that keeps them warm. Other bears have the ability to sleep for long periods of time. In fact, they sleep all winter long. This is called, *hibernation*.

The Bear as a Predator

Did you know that some meat-eating bears stalk their prey? Polar bears like to hunt seals and will wait by a hole in the ice for a seal to come up for air. Once the seal surfaces, the hungry bear grabs it with its powerful jaws and teeth. This bear also hunts for fish in the icy Arctic waters.

The Bear as Prey

Did you know bears have no natural enemies except man? Bears are hunted for their meat and for their thick fur. In some cultures, the bear is hunted for its gall bladder. This is used in some traditional medicines. Bears are also hunted for trophies to hang on someone's wall.

Bear Talk

Did you know that bears can communicate? Some bears will growl and roar when they are angry. Bears can make a huffing sound when they are attracting a mate. They can even bark or moan when they are feeling stressed. Bears will also rub on trees to leave their scent behind.

Mom and Babies

Did you know the mother bear can have anywhere between one to three cubs? The cubs are born hairless, blind and helpless. Baby bears nurse milk from their mothers. Most bear cubs stay with their mom for around three years. She will teach them how to hunt for food and to stay safe.

Bears at Rest

Did you know bears are active all times of the day? Bears will sleep when they get tired and move about looking for food when they are hungry. If bears are living near a busy city, they may come out more at night to stay safe. Bears will rest in and under trees when they want to sleep.

Bears at Play

Did you know bears like to play? Just like you and I, bears will roll around on the ground, run, tumble and play with each other as cubs. Adult bears will splash in the water and rub their backs on trees when they have an itch. Baby bears also learn valuable hunting skills through play.

Life of a Bear

Did you know some bears don't find a mate until they are around nine years-old? Baby bears do most of their growing with their moms, then they leave to live alone. When the bear is mature enough, it will find a mate. Most bears can live to be around 25 years-old.

Grizzly Bear

The Grizzly bear is large and can weigh up to 800 pounds. It is found in North America. It has thick brown fur that is sometimes tipped with white. This bear has a large hump on its back. Grizzlies also like to stand in streams to hunt the salmon as they spawn upstream.

Polar Bear

The Polar bear is the largest of all the bears. Adults can weigh around 1700 pounds and measure 10 feet long. This bear lives in the Arctic regions and hunts seal and fish. It has a thick white coat and black skin. Its skin helps it absorb heat from the sun to keep it warm.

Sun Bear

Also called the Honey bear, the Sun bear is the smallest of all the bear species - it only weighs 100 pounds! It can be found in Southeast Asia. It is black with a U-shaped, yellowish patch of fur on its chest. This bear likes to eat lizards, small rodents, birds and termites.

Quiz

Question 1: How many species of bear are there?

Answer 1: There are 8 species of bear

Question 2: Bears like to eat some plants, what else do they eat?

Answer 2: Insects, seal, fish, nuts, berries and people's garbage

Question 3: When some bears sleep all winter long, what is this called?

Answer 3:Hibernation

Question 4: How does a bear communicate?

Answer 4: Growls, snorts, moans, huffing, barking and scent marking

Question 5: What is the largest bear in the world?

Answer 5: Polar bears. They can weigh up to 1,700 pounds!

Thank you for checking out another addition from Sandie Lee Books! Make sure to check out Amazon.com for many other great titles.